Symphony Upon My Soul

Poems by

Amy Alcini

Amy Alcini

Symphony Upon My Soul/Amy Alcini

ISBN-13: 978-0615898469
ISBN-10: 0615898467

SULBY HALL
PUBLISHERS

USA: PO Box 6867
Malibu CA 90264

Canada: 28 Duncannon Drive,
Toronto ON M5P 2M1

www.sulbyhall.com

love@recyclinghappiness.com
www.recyclinghappiness.com
www.facebook.com/recyclinghappiness

Cover photo by Amy Alcini
Printed in the United States of America

Symphony Upon My Soul

All the love you have received and all the love you have shared
is with you now.
Appeal to your heart and appeal to Heaven,
for you are the vessel God has chosen to change the mind of
this world—
from fear,
back into the eternal imprint of all things:
Love only.

~ Amy Alcini

Amy Alcini

Contents

The Agreement 1

The River 2

Etching Upon My Soul 3

The Darkness 4

Modern Times 6

To You I Owe This Thanks 8

The Vision 9

Lovers 10

One 12

Love Flowing Through 14

Each Other We Long To See 16

Melting In 18

Message From Above 20

What You've Been Brought 22

Our Limitless Power of Love 24

Two Leaves 23

Allowed To Be 27

Choosing To Be 28

Symphony Upon My Soul 29

Train Your Love 30

Our True Intelligence 32

Stillness While In Motion 34

Sentientkind 35

The Lightness of Love 36

The Prophet's Way 38

Amy Alcini

The Agreement

The agreement is to remain in love with you,
bringing our shreds of darkness to light.
The agreement is to lie though silence unknown,
and find Truth in illusion we share.

The agreement is to remain awake—
in the hour of our sorrow,
and bear witness into what is
Love Only.

And the agreement is to Know,
no matter how far we roam,
it's my heart—
that will never know the distance.

Amy Alcini

The River

My heart had become heavy,
a narrowed river,
through sorrow—
an unyielding way.

Then my beloved I met you,
a blessing beyond what I can say,
you smoothed out its edges—
lightened its pass,
you gave it a name of its own.

You provided conviction—
filled it with Love,
opened a place I call home.

Now this river flows sacred,
blessed and Holy—
well beyond its banks,
today I feel the wild ecstasy it holds—
to you I own this thanks.

Etching Upon My Soul

From deep love I cry,
in deeper grief—
I long for my beloved,
who brings me to reverie,
hours escaping—
repeatedly dissolving,
drifting our noons into nights.

Time I saved in Love with you,
I spend in sensitivity—
receiving your love
I lost all me—
in ecstasy,
in joy,
in you,
in me.

And then I watched,
in wonder, amazed—
as you etched upon my soul,
I knew then it was—
now and forever,
my eternity was gently made.

Amy Alcini

The Darkness

Ah, the darkness of human finally revealed
as the mask for which it is,
our minds are convinced—
to make us think,
it's darkness that leaving the scar.

Alas my love—this is illusion,
and how we feed its flame.
Truth lies deeper than the act itself,
but in the fuel behind the flame.

So, shift your perception
and answer the call,
from the One who is already free—
exit this world now while in motion,
and give up your dregs,
To Be.

Loosen your grip from these shackles of mind,
and enter your knowledge beyond—
so close you can taste it,
in Love,
with the wave of your wand.

It's here the darkness,
provides your wounds,

the Light—
in which to see,
responding with Love,
unconditional like grace,
and heals your heart with ease.

Amy Alcini

Modern Times

Yield to temperance,
in these modern times

Awaken,
Divine Will—
come to pass.

Today is the day to shelve ambition,
replacing inspiration—ahead in its path.
As humble we serve, our course to stay,
falling in Love is winning the day.

Called to our Cause—live it well,
by pen and example we lead,
may the breath of Divine—
we contain,
like vessels of Providence
leading our way.

So here we go—into the heart,
ecstatic—abundance of souls,
each one to play the precious note,
sounding in chord as One.

Symphony Upon My Soul

I pray into these modern times
we think the thoughts of Love.
Like Nature we are given—
from immortal we flow,
in generosity,
gifted from above.

Amy Alcini

To You I Owe This Thanks

In the precious years of life I've been given,
to whom I owe this thanks?
It's you who's remained forever my guide,
Divine, your path within.

I am rich beyond treasure,
in ease without care—
because in Love,
with you I'm tied.

Through abundance of earth,
your crystalline of Heaven,
in the plentiful play of your day—
coming to us like a gentle spring rain,
covering your oceans and forests the same—
through your delicate gills,
your genius in blossom—
your generous nature of heart.

Now I rest unending,
to this gratitude of moment,
in the Holy Divine of your days,
through summer blue skies,
and winter chair rocking,
unconditional — the Love you gave.

The Vision

Awe to have the vision,
of what you see in me,
thank you for this picture,
my Love—
from your eyes which I see.
This treasure you've shared,
from your vulnerable heart,
unveiling my future to be.

Your vision, your longing,
your wisdom complete,
to feel these words off your lips—
makes soul leap,
deep inside the beauty—
of what it is you Know,
I follow this vision you see in me—
and through your nutrients,
I grow.

Amy Alcini

Lovers

When I feel the gravitas,
how deeply we dared,
convicted into Love;
my mind goes drifting,
then to current—
in emotion,
cascading from above.

Though our yesterdays seem,
only a dream—
they're with us all the same.
For someday we'll see beyond the veil,
where our Truth was beautifully made.

Bypassing the mind and soaring on air—
may we rest,
in the nests,
of our hearts.
To share this Love—
found,
complete,
and among the Awe of what's to be.

Intimate imagination,
our Love it hovered,
in places—past bliss could compare,

it was my Love, indeed beyond,
this world—of frivolous cares.

I know you know how I feel—
you've told me in your kiss,
smiling in softness,
lingering on lips,
feeling True Love,
watching your glimpse.

It was Love we wrapped
into un-cornered boxes,
that danced upon ribbon of days,
greeting the sun half-past noon
while lingering in paths newly made.

Where we laughed with Divine,
and dined in our Sacred—
while Heaven with reverie watched,
perhaps to feel—our Love created,
that's now it longs to make.

Amy Alcini

One

From snail in shell,
to song of bird,
together we thrive as One.
Creator gives us in every breath,
through Nature—is how it's done.

Riding the back of butterfly's wing,
while whispering leaves of grass—
breathing the Argon,
of God's blue air—
Gandhi, Jesus,
Mohammed, Moses,
You and Rumi the same!

Our worldview One,
and together we are,
in quadrant to shift our map—
from the one that's uncertain,
to the one that is Sacred—
as God gathers us to her lap.

Let us rejoice and feel our connection,
ecstatic in passion we go—
guiding us back onto the path,
into origins of life—we Know.
Where heart's in thought—

Love's embodied,
no need for space or time.

So, open your wings,
to your courage of heart—
because Love,
as One—
can fly.

Amy Alcini

Love Flowing Through The Streets

Last night I had a dream,
of new world order—
where Life—
was the first principle
of all.

Love was flowing through the streets,
and The Holy Spirit—had been called.
Where every person and nation agreed,
to cease from causing harm.

Alas, I saw a new world order,
emerging from The Heavens,
inspired by Love—
from the compassion of many,
protecting every corner.

Humanity our President,
education her Vice—
elected unanimously that day.
where Truth was sacred,
Love abound,
and what was said—
was meant to say.

Symphony Upon My Soul

People flourishing
to their heart's favorite song,
what the world needed most—
towards their spirit they longed.

The ones who'd most suffered,
beyond compare—
now thriving in joy and plenty.

Where everyone gave to those in need,
because we Knew,
it was our insurance of many.

And then I woke into my dream,
to find a new world order.
Now I see—Love flowing through streets,
and crossing every illusionary border....

Amy Alcini

Each Other, We Long To See.

We have a life to live,
in greatness we shall lead,
in life of work we find our Cause,
providing our ministry to be.

Dispelled from fear,
we find our Truth,
superfluous now,
a life of greed.

Our Mirrors reflect,
the illusions we hold
so pray they shatter to pieces—
that we may see,
our Love within,
and far
beyond
theses
worldly
reaches....

Then let us meet—
inside God's mind,
that's called the space between;
where I Know myself

Symphony Upon My Soul

in reflection of your eyes,
it's each other,
we long to see.

Amy Alcini

Melting In

My lips gently part
to find yours the same—
through simplicity,
and ease of soul.

Our melting hearts inward,
tangled as One—
in knowledge we dare to Know.

Soul awaken from shackles of mind,
and this melting continues to rise—
surging to skin,
short hairs to stand,
in longing,
ecstasy,
delight and surprise.

I pray you feel,
this Primary Cause,
in the pulse of your mornings—
in the still of your pause,
that bathe your dreams,
ignite.

In blessing we've tasted,
the marks of Salvation,

where hearts are gently saved,
my lips upon yours,
melting in—
where Love,
and Truth are made.

Amy Alcini

Message From Above

Be not afraid,
for this my love,
is your passage in—
surrender all illusions,
and you shall find—
the treasures I bestow.

Love with conviction,
for the deeper you carve,
the greater the light you shall hold.

You are my love—
the unbridled thought,
that's gently upon my mind.
Remember our connection—
and you shall find,
the grace that moves your soul.

Let go of your trapped body of past,
and release your ego to me,
to feel the present—
this Holy instant,
in the vow of you and me.

This my love—is your Love,
that's changing hearts and minds,

a multiplier of force—so ecstatic and rare,
that all the world—will stop and stare,
and my only request
is to dwell in your heart,
because convicted in Love—
we are never apart.

Amy Alcini

What You've Been Brought

Nay, you are your skin or bones,
personality or question of thought—
eternally Divine,
your are more than this,
turn inward—
to what you've been brought.

Listen to the voice inside it all,
and ask that voice to begin.
Trust in your Knowledge—
because you are my love,
living impressionism of art.

So, Saunter in sunset,
cascade with stream,
because you hold—
the helm to your heart.

You the One,
your assignment chosen—
it's you who's called to lead;
so put on your hat—
and roll up your sleeves,

Creator has said,
there is no more you need.

No time to waste—
in another's thought,
the key to the soul is yours!

Be true in conviction—
and Love through no-condition,
in the unimaginable generosity—
you've been brought.

Amy Alcini

Our Limitless Power of Love

Born we are mystics,
longing towards love,
because Love—is what we are.

So it makes perfect sense,
our lives they lean—
towards Perfect Love not far.

By tending towards self we finally see,
the idea, God's mind,
she thought us be.

The arch is long,
and gently it bends,
to illuminate Love's path—
as it tends,
to land us in regions of heart.

Our Limitless power
of Love my friend,
through the courage of heart,
we find God's way.

Two Leaves

Consider this leaf connected to limb—
and limb connected to tree,
notice her joy and sense of ease,
free to move and sway as she please.

In winds of design, intention from Love,
she plays with her brothers all day—
sun-drenches she glistens
in the winds of joy,
smiling—the miracle,
she is made!

At dusk she shelters among the rest,
protected by God alone—
then venerable and frail,
awakens to morning,
to find and greet you with smile.

Yet not far away, I see her brother,
lying gently by side of the road,
unbending with thirst,
separate from Source—
longing for life, once known.

I bend to lift, his crumpled spine,
and carry him back to his tree—

Amy Alcini

returning him to Love forever,
that I pray now—
he never shall leave.

Allowed To Be

When is the day you'll stop to say,
I'm simply allowed to be.
To allow your beauty,
into the pause—
that replaces illusions of time?

My Love don't you see,
the magnetic the pull—
from your Divine alone,
is enough to keep,
the planets in gravity.

For when you stop,
and allow, yourself to be—
in the full presence,
of your Sacred essence,
you are give our Creator,
the Cause to say,
Thank you!
in Awe and wonder,
of the beauty—she hath made!

Amy Alcini

Choosing To Be

I'm ready to blossom,
I'm ready to bloom!
And then I dared to ask...

I woke in the morning—
and fell to my knees,
new ears in which to hear your Grace,
new eyes in which to see.

In Truth that leans,
to touch the heart—
my soul expanded that day,
to feel the cries—my brother beyond,
from oceans and mountains away.

Now I pause—
and feel The Pulse,
in Love—
you've shared with me.
And I no longer ask,
who I am—

I AM.

Choosing to be!

Symphony Upon My Soul

White cap rolling—
convicted you crash,
with mist upon your crest.

My hands reach out,
to touch your shape—
your Dharma's upon my chest.

Your surface it glistens,
your prescience wise,
reflecting blue embers—
blazing from sky.

Your vastness noble—
consistency rare,
to explore your expanse,
and weightless I bear.

Where, your beginning?
How do you end?
And when was the first—
that you rolled?
As I watch through light—
and listen at night,
to your voice—
splashing symphony, upon my soul.

Amy Alcini

Train Your Love

Train your Love,
don't cloud your light—
keep it clear,
and brilliantly bright.

All the world,
it prays for you joy,
so don't seek,
your brief despair.

Share the beauty,
upon your heart—
it's the size,
of a thousand oceans.

Between your step,
and at your feet—
in clarity,
with crystalline focus.

Go forth my love—
and contain your Sacred,
through your brilliant gift of soul.

Train your Love,
from now to forever,

Symphony Upon My Soul

and my heart—
you always shall hold.

Amy Alcini

Your True Intelligence

It's your true intelligence,
that remembers, your intimacy—
connection of birth.

From a blueprint we're gifted,
effortless to follow,
through heart—
that's closer than near.

Your intelligence Divine—
and lives for Purpose,
to Love—and functions in ease,
to awaken—imagination,
and enlighten the cells,
into the night, the heart—
where she dwells!

She's your loyal friend—
faithful in Truth,
with a purpose
to bathe and delight,
shifting us back two by two—
in passion meant to incite.

This is bliss,
uncertainty and Knowing,
true intelligence,
is Love my friend
that asks us simply—
Behold!

Amy Alcini

Stillness While In Motion

This is the state,
God's hummingbird—
teaching her delicate ways,
bypassing this world,
into the sublime—
through her brilliance,
wings in maze.

I'm lost in her reverie,
of subtle presence,
her grace—
it calms my mind,
she inspires in light,
and dazzles by sight,
while riding—
God's currents,
of air.

Meanwhile I pray,
may we meet in her murmur,
and gently become,
her pause—
transporting us back,
to Nature's grace—
and may eternally here,
we stay.

Sentient-Kind

Love is paramount,
while happiness temporal—
Love endures,
beyond waves of sound—
synapse of thought,
phenomena—
or matter of fact.

Love, our primary code complete,
genetic perceptions we greet—
salient in emotion—enchanting desire,
like particle merges with wave.

For connection we long,
in rhythm we beat—
how Blessed my brother,
and Sentient-Kind.

Amy Alcini

The Lightness of Love

It feels like a bubble,
ready to rise—
from bottom of a boiling kettle,
the lightness of Love,
begins inside,
then gently propels—
us to ride.

Remember my love,
it hears your call—
and Knows all your thoughts
on their way.

It remembers your voice,
that goes unspoken,
recalling your dreams,
through night and day.

This lightness of Love,
is loving you—
so live in joy,
and take the ride!

Because your grace,
and your beauty,
your Love,

and your laughter—
that Cause you gently,
to rise!

Amy Alcini

The Prophet's Way

The way of the prophet,
is the way of the sacred,
living though us, the lives of all—
yes it's reserved, for the lover, the mystic,
of which—you are today!

It comes to us, who answer the call—
we're keepers of his flame;
that illuminates gently, our Heaven on earth—
where Holy,
Love is made.

If any religion stands in the way—
of you and the love of your brother,
believe it not—for never there was,
separation, you from another.

You are the vessel that animates this world,
your joy—the essence of Life.
Your shell is Divine, celebrate—containing,
your brilliance in heart and mind!

It was Jesus who said, when people they saw,
it was then they would believe.
So, watch this blessed light of your life—
it's glowing beneath your feet.

Symphony Upon My Soul

Breathe in love, exhale the rest—
that illusion, attempts to hold,
it's love that takes us—from here to ourselves,
that Spirit begs us to Know.

Take this now,
and go to the world—
sharing your Prophet of Soul,
precious as all the life on earth—
      is the love,
      your heart
    it holds.

Amy Alcini

About The Author

Amy Alcini is the founder and CEO of Recycling Happiness, entrepreneur, musician and poet.

As a former WTA professional tennis player, Amy holds twenty USTA National Tennis Championship titles, and two ITF/USTA World titles representing The USA in Young Cup Team competition. As well she has earned six, #1 end of the year USTA National Rankings from 2000-2102.

Amy lives in Malibu, California with her puppy named Rumi.

www.ingramcontent.com/pod-product-compliance
Lightning Source LLC
Chambersburg PA
CBHW030307030426
42337CB00012B/623